I0138519

Reverberations

回声

Reverberations

回声

Zhang Meng

translated by

Ouyang Yu

PUNCHER & WATTMANN

© Zhang Meng 2022

Translation © Ouyang Yu 2022

This book is copyright. Apart from any fair dealing for the purposes of study and research, criticism, review or as otherwise permitted under the Copyright Act, no part may be reproduced by any process without written permission. Inquiries should be made to the publisher.

First published in 2022
Published by Puncher and Wattmann
PO Box 279
Waratah NSW 2298

http://www.puncherandwattmann.com
web@puncherandwattmann.com

NATIONAL
LIBRARY
OF AUSTRALIA

A catalogue entry for this book is available from the National Library of Australia.

ISBN   9781922571373

Cover design by Morgan Arnett
Printed by Lightning Source International

Contents

萝	9	Lo
完整的寂静	11	Total Stillness
盛夏	13	High Summer
风停了	15	The Wind Has Stopped
后马村	17	Back Horse Village
黑麋峰	19	The Black Elk Peak
冬日	21	On a Winter Day
一只鸟停在树桩上	23	A Bird Perched on a Tree Stump
叹息	25	Sighing
旧词	27	Old Words
轻醒	29	Lightly Awake
想念	31	Missing
一个梦	33	A Dream
偏僻记	35	Keeping Account of the Remoteness
母亲节突然想起某个夜晚	37	I Suddenly Recalled a Particular Night on Mother's Day
穿过乌鲁木齐北路	39	Going Across Urumqi North Road
但	41	But
换气	43	A Change of Air
折痕	45	The Folds
花园	47	In the Garden
摩挲	49	Gently Stroking
消息	51	News
卸下	53	Unloading
秋虫吟	55	The Chanting of Autumn Insects
雨桔	57	The Rain Orange
91 号 101	59	101, No. 91
在羞涩的阴影里	61	In the Shadow of Shyness
水开了	63	The Water Is Boiling Now
晚安，夜的城	65	Good Night, the City of the Night

脸	67	Face
夜晚的猜测学	69	Guesswork at Night
蚱蜢	71	The Grasshopper
孤悬	73	Suspended in Solitude
慢	75	Slow
夜晚的仪式	77	The Night's Ritual
羞涩的枝头背对着风的方向	79	The Shy Branches Had Their Backs towards the Wind
辨	81	Making Out
黑桦树	83	The Black Birch
醒	85	Awake
降临	87	The Fall
未知的旅程	89	An Unknown Journey
他一定后悔自己已经自杀了	91	He Must Have Wished That He Should Not Have Committed the Suicide
人类的孩子	93	A Kid of Mankind
活着的骨头架	95	A Living Frame of Bones
抓拍	97	A Snapshot
蜣螂	99	The Dung Beetle
笼罩	101	Shrouding
先锋……话题……继续	103	The Avant-Garde…the Topic…Continued
蹲	105	Squatting
死亡的气息穿窗而来	107	Breaths of Death Were Coming through the Windows
回声	109	Reverberations
野茱萸	111	The Wild Evodia
296 号	113	No. 296
黑枝条	115	Black Bough
散漫	117	Discursive
秀水弄 1 号	119	No. 1, Xiushui Lane
醒来	121	Waking Up

漫长的午后	123	A Long Afternoon
消失	125	Disappearance
跳闸	127	A Blown Fuse
拎	129	Picking Up
阻力	131	Resistance
掏	133	Grabbing
吃诗	135	Eating Poetry
蚊子	139	The Mosquito

萝

她就是我房间里的
小萝莉
这个夏天，长势疯
狂得超乎想象
她挣破
压抑的诅咒
从书架上垂下来
那是一种魔术
越过了春
天的障眼法
她的娇
嫩亮了立秋后
不动声色的静默
最俏皮的
是她穿过书架背后
竹帘的缝
隙，只等我
一推门
就和她迎面
遇上

Lo

She is the little Lo
lita in my room
this summer, her growth so cra
zy it's beyond imagination
she broke through
the oppressive curse
hanging down the bookcase
a magic
that went across the blind spot of s
pring
her delica
teness lit up the calm silence
after the Start of Autumn
what was most cool
was the fact that she went through the sea
ms in the bamboo curtain
behind the bookcase, waiting to kiss
me
as soon as I pushed the door
open

完整的寂静

黄昏静得只剩树影
有那么一阵
我专心于观察它移动的力量
感受内心另一片阴影
偏移的

倔强。几乎每天
都要面对这样的时刻
风卷起叶子，鸟安于静寂
林子里什么都有
都在悄悄调整
迎接夜晚

的心。我无法测出
那朵云
与阳台的距离
如同无法说出这
完整的寂静

Total Stillness

The evening was so still only tree shadows were left
for a time
I focussed on observing the power of their movement
feeling for the stubbornness
of another shadow in my heart

as it shifted. Nearly every day
I have to face such moments
in which the wind curls the leaves and the birds are comfortable with
the stillness
there's everything in the wood
and they are all quietly adjusting
to welcome the heart

of the night. I am not able to measure
the distance between that cloud
and the balcony
the same way I'm not able to speak out the
total stillness

盛夏

我坐在阴凉的丝瓜棚下
我放走了一条迷路的蛇
不想见到的人准时又经过门前
我获得了一只鹅的赞许
我总是被蝉声催眠
我行走在水洼明亮的土路上
月光类似散淡的盐，乡间的盐
我的老邻居在百岁来临之前
每晚痛哭死去的老伴
我常梦见在那棵古银杏下醒来
它凹凸的树皮比史书厚
秋风在芦苇荡里巡游
几十年后，那里除了白鹭
还有新鲜的野兔脚印，在露水里
在清晨薄凉的鸟声里
我游离在石桥和潮声之间
我吹奏无人听懂的苇声
我丢失我自己，唤醒
另一个自己

可是，我在一座电影院里

High Summer

I was sitting beneath a cool loofah shed
I had let go of a strayed snake
the one I didn't want to see went past my door on time again
I had won praise from a goose
I am always eased into sleep by the sound of cicadas
I walk on the earthen road with bright puddles
moonlight like flat salt, salt in the country
my old neighbour, prior to the coming of his centennial
cries for his dead partner every night
I often dream of the ancient gingko that wakes up
its bulgy bark thicker than a history book
the autumn wind was cruising in the reeds
decades after, there are fresh footprints of wild rabbits
apart from those of the egrets, and in the dews
and the thin birdcalls in the early mornings
I wander between the stone bridge and the sound of the tide
I blow the sound of a reed that defies understanding
I've lost myself, having woken up
another self

but, I am in a cinema

风停了

风趴下时
我才看清它疲惫的模样
擦着巷口传来的
清亮口哨，突然消失
它贴着一片卷曲的
叶子，喘息平缓
如叶片般
放松开来，舒展
开来，它停下
类似一枚绿蜻蜓
落在荷叶上
翅膀带动
若隐似荡的细小
波纹。没有人
注意到它是怎么
停下来的
它可能是听从了某种
神秘的指示
急促、悄然，领受安静
的命途

The Wind Has Stopped

It's not till the wind lay face down
that I saw the features of its fatigue
the clear whistle that came scraping
the mouth of the lane disappeared on a sudden
as it lay stuck to a curled up
leaf, breathing evenly
loosened up
like the leaf, spread
open, and it paused
like a green dragonfly
perched on a lotus-leaf
its wings stirring
the half-visible
ripples. No one
noticed how it
paused
it might have followed a certain
mysterious instruction
by accepting the fortune of quietness
in a rapid and quiet manner

后马村

青色的野柿子挂满枝头
雨水打湿的脸庞泛出
一丝红晕
它椭圆形的样子
让我们猜不出名字。在后马村
一场细雨清洗着人去楼空的静
后马村189号，沧桑的门牌在风中摇晃
92岁的老奶奶
和一棵干瘪的树，站在细雨中
我心里有一种说不清的空
山岚一样升起
我被空塞满
也被空放空
我找不到流水的源头
就像找不到后马村
清晰的来处
旧居颓败，木板散乱成时光留下的灰
我惊讶于浙东群山环抱里
一个空了心的山村
影射着一个时代溃烂的病症
而破败的正在破败
矗立的正在矗立

Back Horse Village

The wild green persimmons were hanging all over the branches
their rain-drenched faces
reddish
and their oblong shapes
made it impossible for us to guess their names. In Back Horse Village
a drizzle was washing the quietness of a deserted place
No. 189, its number plate of vicissitudes swaying in the wind
old grandma, aged 92
and a shriveled tree, stood in the drizzle
there was an unspeakable hollowness in my heart
that was rising like a mist in the mountains
I was filled with hollowness
and emptied by it, too
I wasn't able to find the source of the running water
the same way I wasn't able to find the clear origins of
Back Horse Village
old residences dilapidated, wooden boards scattered like the dust
time had left
I was taken aback by a heart-hollowed mountain village
in the arms of the eastern Zhejiang mountains
that reflected the ills of a rotten age
while the ruins are being ruined
buildings are also being built

黑麋峰

奔跑。跃动。像一切生灵的神
我想象中的黑麋鹿是一首远方的诗

惊慌失措地回首，在一棵树丫旁
双眼清澈，闪电般慌张

山谷里，或者矮坡间，雨后蘑菇
潮润的湿气恰如其分

想象中的远方，就是满山苍郁
就是农舍隐匿山腰，炊烟袅然成云

黄昏时，一路循着黑麋鹿的踪迹走去
远处隐约传来瀑布声

The Black Elk Peak

Running. Leaping. Like a god of all creatures
the black elk in my imagination is a faraway poem

he, in panic, looks back, by the side of a bough
his eyes clear, as flurried as a lightning

in the valley, or between the low slopes, the after-rain mushrooms
had an appropriate moisture

the imaginary distance was a mountain of verdure
peasant cottages hidden in the waist of it, with wisps of smoke
                                        turning into clouds

at dusk, when you trace the spoor of the elk all the way
you may hear the faint sound of a fall in the distance

冬日

几个男人围在墙角
闷声抽着烟
孝服像刚落下的一场雪

小河边，芦苇枯成一片
万物轮回，该凋谢的
已凋谢，该发芽的正在发芽

积雪未化，泥泞的小路上不时有人进来
场院里搭起了简易的帐篷
送别的队伍越来越大

空落落的鸟巢里
几片羽毛被风卷起
又缓缓落下

On a Winter Day

Men were in a corner
smoking, in silence
their mourning clothes resembling the fallen snow

by the side of the small river, the reeds had withered
things, in the wheel of fortune, which should have gone dead
had gone dead, or were sprouting if they felt like sprouting

the snow was yet to melt and there were occasional visitors along the
                                              muddy path
a slapdash tent was erected in the courtyard
and the funeral procession was growing longer

a few feathers were being blown
out of the empty bird's nest
before they slowly fell, again

一只鸟停在树桩上

远远看见一只鸟
停在木桩上
羽毛在阳光下发出七彩的光
一声翠绿的叫声
吸引了我，它停在那里
仿佛是从一截木桩里
长出的花
让这个萧瑟的午后
多了一丝亮色

可我叫不出它的名字
此刻，一片安静
阳光撒在废弃已久的
荒地上
在夏天，野草
曾疯狂吞噬过它，现在
冬至将近
在突然降临的寒潮里

A Bird Perched on a Tree Stump

I saw a bird in a distance
perched on a tree stump
its feathers sending forth seven-coloured lights
and its green cry
attracting me, it stopped there
like a flower
grown out of the stump
adding a bright colour
to this bleak afternoon

but I didn't know its name
right now, quiet
sunshine was spreading itself across the abandoned
wasteland
in the summer, wild weeds
had crazily swallowed it and now
the winter solstice was coming
in the cold wave that had just arrived

叹息

最后一丝光线
透过屋顶照在船头的铁锚上
内心锈蚀。但
一定还有波涛的回声
在涌动

从镜头里看去
这个天然小渔港
比一幅刚完成的油画
更生动
色彩浓重，裹着强烈的冲击力

船静泊
盐质记忆里储满蔚蓝色鱼群
风贴着中年的心跳
沉在心底的锚
正发出低沉的叹息

Sighing

The last ray of light
was shed on the iron anchor on the bow, through the roof
a rusty heart of hearts. But
there must be the echoes of waves
surging

seen from the lens
this natural little harbour
was more vivid
than an oil painting, just completed
with rich colours, carrying with it a strong impact

boats quietly moored
salty memories filled with blue schools of fish
the wind close to the heartbeats of middle age
the anchor, sunken to the bottom of the heart
was sighing in a low voice

旧词

黑夜是一口敞开的过滤器
又一天走到尽头
摸黑中拐进乌鸦色的巷口

——月光的拐角处，一眼老井
映出陈旧的星辰
风来自树枝，带走的每一片落叶

月亮是秋天的旧物
在一盏灯下，失眠者
翻寻着月光遗落的线索

清晨醒来
看着镜子里的脸：一枚
昨天的旧词

Old Words

Dark night is an open filter
another day gone to its end
groping its way in the dark, to the mouth of the black-magpie-
coloured lane

—at a corner of the moonlight, an old well
reflected the old stars
the wind came out of every fallen leaf, taken away by the branches

the moon was an old thing of the autumn
beneath a lamp, the insomniac
was ransacking the clues left by the moonlight

in the early morning when I woke up
I saw my face in the mirror: an
old word from yesterday

轻醒

夜里
因为轻微的声响醒来
好几次都是这样
睡梦里
有个遥远的声音在响起
像隔着一座山
风拍打残枝
墨色的声音窸窸窣窣
落叶飘到河面
轻微的声音
荡开在夜色里
我听到轻微脚步声
吸引着我的脚步
前方是哪里
翻山越岭之后
又将是哪里
夜里
因为轻微的声响醒来
黑暗中
摸摸真实的心跳
久久无法入睡

Lightly Awake

At night
I woke up because of a light sound
on quite a few occasions
in my dream
a distant sound arose
as if separated by a mountain
the wind slapped the remnant branches
as the inky sound was soughing
fallen leaves drifted to the river
and a light sound
was dispersed in the colours of the night
I heard the light footsteps
attracting my footsteps
where is it ahead of me?
where will it be
after I climb mountain after mountain?
at night
I woke up because of a light sound
in the darkness
I touched my real heartbeats
unable to fall back into sleep for a long time

想念

在石屋想念风石
在海边想念琵琶
在海上想念桅杆
在露台想念岛屿
在井边想念星光
在山脚想念奶奶
在屋檐想念蜘蛛
这些
都还不够诗味
我最喜欢那一句
"在东京想念东京"

Missing

In the stone house I miss the wind stone
at the seaside I miss the lute
at sea I miss the masts
on the balcony I miss the island
at the side of the well I miss the starlight
at the foot of the hill I miss my granny
at the eaves I miss the spider
but none of these
is poetic enough
as the best line I love is
'In Tokyo I miss Tokyo'

一个梦

我一定是睡着了
你看，我多么安静
躺在秋天的怀抱里
妈妈说，秋日的阳光
也是暖洋洋的
可我怎么
一点也感觉不到
它们就这么静静地洒
在我身上
风很细
从我耳边走过，我奓拉着的
左耳朵
可能轻微地动了一下
又轻轻地
搁在一粒小石子上
哦，世界
静得像一个梦
我躺在马路中央
像躺在
世界的中央
橘黄色的尾巴
多么好看
一动不动地
压在住了双黄线
全然不顾
潮水般来往的车流

A Dream

I must have fallen asleep
you see how quiet I am
lying in the arms of the autumn
Mother said: even the sunlight of the autumn
is warm
but why didn't I
feel it?
I didn't feel it at all
it was quietly shed
on me
the wind was thin
walking past my ears, my drooping
left ear may have slightly moved
before it lightly
settled itself on a tiny stone
oh, the world
was as quiet as a dream
I lay down in the middle of the road
like in
the middle of the world
my orange tail
so pretty
lying across the double-yellow line
without motion
completely ignoring
the tides of traffic

偏僻记

树木和灌木丛
都被覆盖在一层
毛毛虫似的
寒霜之下
我喜欢
这寒冷的
灰扑扑的假日
租住在
偏僻小屋
花园枯寂无声
用写诗打发漫长
单调的时光
有些事
第一次经历时
会感到新鲜的快乐

Keeping Account of the Remoteness

Trees and the undergrowth
were all covered in a layer
of frost
like caterpillars
I like this
cold
dusty holiday
when I rented
in a remote hut
the garden soundless
where I killed the long
and boring time writing poetry
there were certain things
that you found fresh and enjoyable
when you first experienced them

母亲节突然想起某个夜晚

天暗得很快
我赶到的时候
门还开着
院子里
月色清凉
顺着往里走
我知道你就在里面
轮椅
羁绊了你的脚步
月光的手指太远
它无法为你
按下开关
我边走边喊
我看不清你
黑暗中的样子
你应了一声
像一盏灯
啪地，在心里亮起

I Suddenly Recalled a Particular Night on Mother's Day

The sky darkened quickly
when I hurried to the place
the door was still open
in the courtyard
the colours of the moon were clear and cool
as I walked along inside
I knew you were there
the wheelchair
crippled your footsteps
and the fingers of the moonlight were too far
to press the button
for you
I walked as I cried
as I could not clearly see
the way you looked in the darkness
you made a reply
like a lamp that
with a click, was switched on in my heart

穿过乌鲁木齐北路

四月的空气泛着凉意
高架上车流飞驰
爱城市，同时也要爱它
繁忙的节奏、发动机的轰鸣
尾气的熏陶，以及
满头飞扬的杨絮
穿过乌鲁木齐北路时
街角一个红色电话亭边
一辆破旧的小三轮上
搁着几捆破纸板
两小袋饮料瓶
收废品的人
蜷缩着躺在电话亭里
枕着呼啸的车轮声
睡着了
阳光照在脸上
像个孤独的孩子

Going Across Urumqi North Road

The April air was cool
a flying flow of traffic on the overpass
when you love the city, you must also love
its busy rhythms, the roar of the engines
and the smell of the exhaust pipes, as well as
the poplar catkins circling one's hair
as I went across Urumqi North Road
I saw that by the side of a red telephone booth in a street corner
and on a small ramshackle tricycle
with bundles of used cardboards
and two small bags of drink bottles
a rag-and-bone man
was lying curled up in the booth
asleep on the pillow
of the roaring wheels
the sun was shining on his face
like that of a lonely child

但

透过树枝，我看到什么
除了寂寥
光晕般散开

十二月，空气清冽
四野寂寂，落单的鸟
飞离枝头

深藏的断痕
哆嗦了一下，但，并不
为人所知

But

Through the branches what I saw
except the solitude
that was dispersing itself like an aura?

in December, the air was clean and cold
the fields around were quiet as the single bird
was leaving the branch

the trace of breakage, deeply hidden
shivered, but was not
known

换气

跟着她跳跃的节奏
跟着她闪烁又迷离的气息
跟着她走
跟着她往左转
跟着她往右转
跟着她上坡
跟着她蔑视悬崖
跟着她走
跟着她静听一棵古槐树
跟着她与一个老者的目光对视
跟着她撬动时间的嘴巴
跟着她从一块黑铁里出淬出火花
跟着她走
跟着她飞翔
跟着她潜水
跟着她在诗中学会换气

A Change of Air

following her leaping rhythms
following her air, twinkling and obsessive
following her walk
following her turn left
following her turn right
following her up the slope
following her in her contempt of the cliff
following her walk
following her in quietly listening to an ancient locust tree
following her meeting the eye of an old man
following her prying open the mouth of time
following her tempering a black iron till the fiery flowers burst
following her walk
following her fly
following her dive
following her in how to have a change of air in poetry

折痕

流逝之物固然可惜
——河里的小蝌蚪，树枝上的鸟巢
河流有干涸之殇，残枝
有断臂之痛。那些流逝之声
犹如体内的断骨
——清脆有声

该如何让时光倒流
让草木回到葳蕤盛年，蛙声重返
七月黄昏
如何收藏一座远去的村庄
蝶翅收纳了草木的呼吸
它在草尖上轻轻合拢乡村的诗篇
以及，光阴的折痕

The Folds

It is a pity, for sure, that things flow and disappear
—the tadpoles in the river, the bird's nests in the trees
the river may die prematurely of drought and the remaining branches
may suffer the pain of a broken limb. The sound of all that flows and
disappears
like the broken bones inside the body
—is crisp and loud

how can one allow time to flow backwards
to allow grass and trees to return to their prime and to allow the frog
crows to return
to the July evenings?
and how to collect a village going further away
where the butterfly's wings are storing the breathings of the grass
and trees
as they, on the tips of the grass, are gently closing the poems of the
village
and the folds of time

花园

是的。这里有点杂乱
枯萎的芦荟抽出了新叶
绿色火焰来自肥厚的茎
身体充满戒备，与一丛正拔节的芦苇
保持着安全距离
蔷薇长势狂乱，甩开木栅栏的扶手
一路狂奔
独自开辟了新空间——
事实上，它们已经霸占了花园的大部分领地
蜜蜂偶尔来访
像节日里串门的乡下亲戚
流连花香
而忘了轻敲门扉

In the Garden

Right. It's a bit messy here
the aloe, withered, was sprouting new leaves
and the green fire came from the fat stem
its body on guard, keeping a safe distance
from a cluster of jointing reeds
the roses were growing in wild abundance, rushing all the way
after leaving the handrail on the wooden fence
creating their own new space—
when, in fact, they were occupying much of the garden's territory
bees paid occasional visits
like one's village relatives, visiting on festive occasions
but they were so obsessed with the fragrant flowers
that they forgot to knock on the door

摩挲

风没有停之前
靠着松树，松叶的轰鸣
低沉
树干里
雷电的回音
隐约传入耳膜

年久的干旱
被唤醒
把心沉下来
贴近溪水
听一条河流的
怒吼

手搭大地，蹄声
沿着地面传来
一种血脉喷张的感觉
传到掌心，风摩挲着落叶
发出近于虚
幻的声音

Gently Stroking

Before it stopped
the wind leaned against the pine tree, its leaves were roaring
in a low voice
inside its trunk
the echoes of the thunder and lightning
faintly reached the eardrums

the yearlong drought
sank the wakeful
heart
close to the creek
listening to a river
roaring in anger

when you put your hand on the earth, the sound of the hooves
came from across the ground
a feeling of spurting blood
spread to the heart of the hand as the wind gently stroked the fallen
                                                                            leaves
generating a nearly virtual
sound

消息

一个已经走失好久的人
就像黄昏时出门去散步
忘带了钥匙

一个走着走着就迷路了的人
在与世界隔绝的地方
把森林命名为孤独

不必去找回家的路
锁孔已泅出铜绿色诗行
门缝上也早已长出新鲜的蘑菇

不必知道任何消息了
对于一个在时间裂缝里消逝了的人
没有消息，就是最好的消息

News

For someone who has gone missing for a long time
it feels like going out on a walk at dusk
but forgetting to bring his keys

for someone who has lost his way as he walks
he can name the forest after solitude
in a place separated from the world

it's not necessary to find one's way home
as the keyhole has spread copper-green lines of poetry
and the crack of the door has also grown fresh and new mushrooms

it's not necessary to know of any news
as, for each and every one who has disappeared in the crack of time
no news is the best news

卸下

其实，我只是想找个地方
坐坐
如果有海风吹着
那是最好的

这真是个安静的好地方
惊涛一路赶来
到我脚下时，已停止了
喘息

像一个刚刚卸下斗篷的斗士
舔着我的脚趾
我坐在这里
像夕阳里的一滴墨

遥远的魅惑
早已稀释在海风中
在同一纬度上
我感应着另一颗一起跳动的心

Unloading

In fact, all I wanted is a place
to sit down
it would be best
if there was a blowing sea wind

this is a good place, really quiet
astonishing waves came rushing over all the way
by the time they reached my feet, they had stopped
panting

like a warrior who had just taken off his cloak
and was licking my toes
here sat I
like a blob of ink

the allure from afar
had dissolved in the sea wind
on the same latitude
I was sensing another heart that was beating at the same time

秋虫吟

与你相遇
纯粹是一场秋夜里的意外
歌声滤尽悲怆的沉渣
略带寒气——
浸润着露水的湿脾之症

草丛幽暗，都是你隐秘的宫殿
在这重返的傲慢之气中
有穿破荆棘的窸窣声
变幻的节奏里
隐约分辨出你急迫的耐心

星孤悬，夜晚的航班
穿过苍穹
天地旷远，我渺小如一介秋虫
在紫藤架下坐久了
肩上沾满了露水和星光

The Chanting of Autumn Insects

My encounter with you
was a pure accident on an autumn night
all the dregs of sorrow filtered out of your song
that carried a little chill in it—
moistened with the dewy splenopathy

clusters of gloomy grass were your hidden palace
in this air of arrogance on its return
there was a soughing sound of the brambles being penetrated
and in the changing rhythms
one could vaguely tell of your urgent patience

a star was hanging alone as a night airplane
went through the dome of the sky
the sky, the earth, both far and vast, and I was as tiny as an autumn
insect
when I sat for a long time under the wisteria rack
my shoulders were covered with the light of dew and stars

雨桔

下午因雨的到来
显得有些臃肿
灌好浆的稻田里
一片蚱蜢绿
桔树沉下了身子
挂念太多，有点喘不过气来
每一只饱胀的桔子
已学会如何分泌出阳光
等天晴的时候
它们会慢慢变成金色的
灯笼。废弃的井栏圈
靠在桔树身旁
确切地说
我离它们只有
几米之远，但听不清它们
在渐渐凉下来的秋雨中
说了些什么

The Rain Orange

because of the rain that came
the afternoon seemed a little obese
the rice paddies, filled with water
were grasshopper green
an orange tree, its body bent
had too much concern it was breathless
each and every swollen orange
had learnt how to ooze sunshine
when the weather was fine
they'd slowly turn into golden
lanterns. The disused railings around the well
were leaning against the orange tree
or to be more exact
I was metres away
from them but could not make out what
they were talking about
in the cooling autumn rain

91 号 101

91 号 101——
91 号 101——
送快递的在窗外看到了我
大声喊着

这个时候我正在厨房窗口
整理一把青菜
天太热了，在这之前
我干脆把 T 恤也脱了
赤膊，只套了个简易围兜
像个正在剔猪毛的屠夫

我说你就干脆从窗口递进来吧
他穿过窗外的矮冬青
绕到窗口，当包裹递进来的那一刻
突然让我想起，某部电影里
接头的情景

101, No. 91

101, No. 91——
101, No. 91——
the courier saw me outside the window
and cried out loud

at the time I was sorting out a handful of vegetables
at the kitchen window
it was so hot and before this
I had stripped off my T-shirt
to bare arms, wearing a simple apron
like a butcher scraping off a pig's hair

I said: Can you just put it in through the window?
he circled around the low holly
outside the window and the moment the parcel was passed in
I thought of the scene in a film
where someone makes the first contact with someone else

在羞涩的阴影里

不是羞涩
是在廊柱的阴影里

事物在黄昏后显现黑白影调
微弱的光线打在廊柱上

影子带给我想象和虚构的兴奋
海，在另一边喘息

陌生人在长廊尽头，背影富有诗意
每个夜晚降临，都有意外的美

一切，在廊柱的阴影里
不在羞涩里

In the Shadow of Shyness

Not shyness
but in the shadow of the columns

things, after the dusk, reveal the tones of black and white
as faint light falls on the columns

the shadow brings me the excitement of imagination and fiction
the sea, though, is panting, on the other side

a stranger at the end of the long corridor, the shadow of his back
                                                            poetic
when it falls, every night surprises with its beauty

everything, in the shadow of the columns
not in the shyness

水开了

这么多年了
我仍喜欢在乡村生活里忙碌
尤其喜欢用铝壶
在煤炉上烧水

冬天，院子里积了薄雪
风瘦成刀片
我甩着膀子在一旁劈柴
闻着松木香
心里的春天开始发芽

水壶滋滋地响着
水开了
隔着壶嘴冒出的雾
突然想起那年在北方
坐着火车
穿行在一场大雪中

The Water Is Boiling Now

After so many years
I still like getting busy in my country life
particularly preferring the aluminium kettle
to boil hot water on a coal stove

in winter, there was thin snow in the courtyard
and the wind had thinned into a razor
I chopped the firewood, swinging my arms
and smelling the pinewood
a spring sprouting in my heart

the kettle began sizzling
and the water was boiling
through the fog that came out of the mouth of the kettle
when I suddenly recalled the north that winter
as I was on a train
passing through a big snow

晚安，夜的城

夜幕深
一城灯火在脚下铺开，站在九楼窗台———
俯瞰这倒映的银河
璀璨、迷醉，这人间的灯
这霓虹幻化的星辰

站在巨大的落地窗前，看见自己的倒影。
一张陌生的脸，悬在空中：
星河中升起的脸，路灯在背后伸向远方
车流无声穿梭，这夜晚的鱼群
将游向何方？

病房里，寂静在滴管里走动
每一滴都安抚着虚弱的脉搏。我转身
看着病床上的脸
轻缓的呼吸陷在夜深处，氧气管冒着气泡
鱼群正游进陌生的身体

黑暗中的病房，我孤独如
浮出河面的鱼。晚安
幽暗的窗台。晚安，闪着荧光的
呼吸机
晚安，夜的城

Good Night, the City of the Night

A deep curtain of night
a city of lights spread themselves under me as I stood by the window
on the ninth floor—
looking down on this reflected Silver River
brilliant, intoxicating, the lamps of the world
the stars that the neon had turned into

standing behind the French window, I saw my own reflection
a strange face, hung in the air:
a face that had risen in a river of stars as the road lamps extended
into the distance behind me
the flow of the traffic shuttling, without a sound, but where did this
night's school
of fish swim?

in the ward, quietness was moving in the burette
each drop comforting the weak pulse. I turned around
and saw the face on the sickbed
its gentle and slow breathings sunken into the depths of the night
and where the oxygen tube was bubbling
a school of fish was swimming into a stranger's body

in the dark ward, I was as solitary as
a fish that was coming to the surface of the river. Good night
the gloomy window. Good night, the florescent
breathing machine
and Good night, the City of the Night

脸

一楼的车库
有些低矮
原来是储物用
不知何时
竟住进了人
还装上了不锈钢
防盗小窗
有几次
我隔着窗
望进去
看到一张
格子脸
有时
天气好
他会走到外面
晒太阳
这突然让我想起
某部监狱题材电影里
一张放风的
脸

Face

The garage on the ground floor
is low
it was once used for storage
but no one knows when
someone has checked in
and has installed an anti-theft window
built of stainless steel
on several occasions
I look in
and see a
latticed face
sometimes
when the weather is good
he may come outside
to sun himself
it suddenly puts me in mind of
a prison film
about a face
let out for fresh air

夜晚的猜测学

站在阳台上随意一瞥
看见对面楼梯旁的树枝上
挂着一件衣服
风一吹
就动一下
伸出的袖子
仿佛是和仇家
一次无声的和解
更多时候
它静止不动，双臂垂落在
浓重的夜色里
如果觉得冷
它也无法
抱紧自己
一件挂在疑问里的衣服
让人无端生出
些许猜测

Guesswork at Night

Standing on the balcony and taking a casual glance
I saw a piece of clothing
hanging on a branch next to the opposite building
when the wind blew
it moved
its extended sleeve
like in a silent reconciliation
with an enemy
more often, though
it remained motionless, its arms hanging down
in the heavy darkness
even if it felt cold
it couldn't possibly
hold itself tight
a piece of clothing hanging inside a question
had thus generated
so much guesswork

蚱蜢

是有层次的
和声音一样
蚱蜢振翅的纹路
被季节的轮盘
碾压
走在秋的原野
每一步
都能感到细微的颤
动。轻如一粒
草籽，在风中
抖落。重若闪电的头颅
砸进大地。太多生命
在我们呼
吸的瞬间
陨落。无人感知
在一片半黄
不黄的叶片上
绿蚱蜢
蹬着强劲的后腿
憋足了劲
把自己
射
了出去

The Grasshopper

is layered
like the sound
with the veins of wing-fluttering
ground down
by the wheels of seasons
as I walk on the autumn plain
every step of mine
can feel the lightest shi
ver, as light as a grain
of grass seed, dropping
in the wind, its head, as heavy as the lightning
smashing into the earth. Too much life
has fallen
in the instant
of our breathing that no one has been made aware of
on the blade of a half-yellow leaf
the green grasshopper
shoots
itself out
by pushing its powerful rear legs
bursting with energy

孤悬

只有到过乡村
才懂得夕阳的美
不止一次从这条小路上走过
一晃间
落叶又收藏了春天的脚印

我曾经是个容易迷路的孩子
在乡村的怀抱里得到俗世之暖
在纷扬落叶里
我总是为树枝高处的鸟巢担心
常常抬头看着它

秋风一阵冷过一阵
而暮色在萧瑟的天空盘旋
这孤悬的一家
挤在寒夜里
只有秋风这床薄被单

Suspended in Solitude

Only when you have arrived in a village
can you appreciate the beauty of its sunset
I, though, have walked on this little path more than once
in the twinkling of an eye
the fallen leaves have again collected the footsteps of the spring

I used to be a boy easily led astray
but I gained worldly warmth in the arms of the village
in the scattered fallen leaves
I always worry about the bird's nest in the branches on high
and often raise my head to look at it

the autumn wind is getting colder now
and the colours of the evening are hovering in the bleak sky
the family, suspended in solitude
were huddling together in the cold night
their thin quilt, the autumn wind

慢

听阳光在沙滩散步
听一粒沙摩挲着光的毛边
听时间在塌陷
听风路过身边的脚步
听衣角被翻动了一下
听突然冒出的意念
听心跳
听皱纹在松弛
听礁石的呼吸
听海浪轻拍船舷
听一只贝壳的懒腰
听夕阳顺着桅杆爬下来
听另一个自己在体内走动
听潮汐联通了血液
听一个慢人正在远去

Slow

Listening to the sunlight having a walk on the beach
Listening to a grain of sand stroking the furry edge of the light
Listening to time collapsing
Listening to the footsteps of wind passing by.
Listening to the corner of my clothes being lifted
Listening to the sudden emergence of an idea
Listening to the heart beat
Listening to the wrinkles relax
Listening to the reefs breathe
Listening to the sea waves gently pat the side of the boat
Listening to a shell straighten its back
Listening to the setting sun climb down a mast
Listening to another self moving inside me
Listening to the tide connected with blood
Listening to a slow person going further away

夜晚的仪式

从车里爬出来
踩着农历十二月
的月光和冷
我已忘了
孤独为何物

怅然于作为儿子的部分
如何消融在这月色里
我试着在虚空里
喊着父亲
没有一棵树回答我

忍住悲伤
在夜色里完成这秘密的
仪式
没有人知道
夜空是最隐秘的父亲

The Night's Ritual

Crawling out of my car
and treading on the moonlight and the cold
in lunar December
I already had
forgotten what loneliness was

wondering how to dissolve
my part as a son in the colours of the moon
I tried to call my father
in the air
but not a single tree answered me

I held back my sorrow
completing the secret ritual
in the colours of the night
no one knew, though
the night sky was the most secret father

羞涩的枝头背对着风的方向

篱笆上最后一枚佛手果
摇荡着秋天的铃铛。也摇荡着
一口老水井的孤寂

丝瓜架上的藤蔓网住了一小片天空
我仰头看它的时候，一条老丝瓜的阴影里
斜逸出一朵嫩黄的小花
像一盏秋风忘了提走的灯
柔细的身子撑破正在衰败的院落

安静地坐在一角
听枣树和柿子树在风中的对话
羞涩的枝头背对着风的方向

挂着拐杖的老人从院门口走过
孤独加重了她的脚步
她深深弯下的驼背，不停地向生活鞠着躬——

在秋天面前，沉重的事物
显现出恭顺的一面

The Shy Branches Had Their Backs towards the Wind

The last Buddha's hand fruit over the fence
was shaking the autumn's bell as it shook
the solitude of the old well

the vines on the loofah trellis netted a small sky
when I looked up at them, a small tender-yellow flower
peeped askance out of the shade of an old loofah
like a lantern that the autumn wind had forgotten to take away
its supple body breaking through the courtyard in ruins

quietly, I sat in a corner
listening to the dialogue in the wind between the date tree and the
                                                    persimmon tree
their shy branches having their backs towards the wind

an old woman, with a stick, walked past the entrance
her footsteps heavy with loneliness
she was bent double as she kept bowing towards life—

in front of the autumn, heavy things
presented their humble side

辨

除了其他病痛
母亲的视力
也越来越不好了
要分辨十米外的来人
基本靠声音

对于时间
墙上的钟挂得
有点高
指针在她视线里
已成了模糊的概念

"天井里的阴影盖住
那扇小木窗时，就是下午两点了"
前几天在乡下听她这么说时
我才在时间的阴影里
感受到了她的孤独

Making Out

Apart from her other conditions
mother also had a worsening
vision
to make out someone in a distance of ten metres
she basically had to rely on sound

as for time
the clock on the wall
was a bit too high
its hands in her vision
had become a blurry concept

'When the shadow in the Skywell covers
the small wooden window, it's two o'clock in the afternoon'
it was not till a few days ago when I heard her say so in the village
that I, in the shade of time
realised her solitude

黑桦树

鸟巢瘦成月光下的影子
星辰在头顶行走。永恒的遥远
多么具有吸引力

星光微弱，镶满心底
旷野上，我的根也在地下走动
发光的事物是坚韧的信仰

我喜欢这黑夜里的画布
在纬度和经度间，我用根须丈量
孤独的精度

疏枝斜逸，每一粒
璀璨之光
都是上帝遗落的火种

一生，我都在努力向上
每接近天空一寸
离古老的星辰就近了一步

The Black Birch

The bird's nest has so thinned it becomes a shadow under the
                                                          moonlight
and the stars are walking overhead. The faraway eternity
is so attractive

the starlight is faint, embedded in the bottom of the heart
over the wilderness, my roots are also moving underground
things that shed light are firm belief

I love the canvass of the dark night
between the latitude and longitude, I measure the accuracy
of loneliness with the roots

the sparse branches extend themselves askance, and each grain
of brilliant light
is the kindling stuff left by God

all my life, I have been striving upwards
and, with each inch I get close to the sky
there's one step closer to the ancient stars

醒

风吹落叶
文翔路上的路灯熄灭了
臃肿的城市
开始醒来
鸟声过滤空气
每一棵树
都从梦里抬起头来
半亩方塘
映出黎明的脸
此时站在阳台上
倒影清晰晃动
每天早上,我都要对着它
照一照这张
"半老不老,半嫩不嫩的脸"*
楼下准时传来扫地声
沙沙,沙沙
单调而又动听

*此句引用自欧阳昱诗歌。

Awake

The wind blowing the fallen leaves
and the lights over Wenxiang Road switched off
the obese city
was just waking up
the birdcall was filtering the air
and every tree
was raising its head from the dream
half of a square pond
reflected the face of dawn
as I now stood on the balcony
I saw the swaying of clear reflections
every morning, I'd look into it
to see this
'half old, half-tender face'*
when the sound of the floor being swept came
tsa, tsa, tsa
monotonous and melodious

* A line quoted from a poem by Ouyang Yu.

降临

……而后
寂静降临
我们只是坐在那里
陶醉在波光中
海鸥飞翔，翅膀
掀动水面的光
松树覆盖着岛屿
山峰在远处
升起蓝色的波涛
风突然搅动一片水面
一颗树的倒影
就是寂静的本身
光落在淡紫色的花瓣上
像刚刚降临的祈祷

The Fall

...then
silence fell
we were only just sitting there
intoxicated in the light of the waves
the seagulls were flying, their wings
lifting the light over the water
the pine trees over the island
the mountaintop in the distance
raised the blue waves
the wind, all of a sudden, stirred up the water
the shadow of a tree
was the stillness itself
when the light fell on the purplish flower-petals
it was like a prayer, just fallen

未知的旅程

二十年转眼过去
我还是很怀念那条铁轨
梦中的铁轨
在八福洞郊外 *

记得那些盛夏的傍晚
我常坐在那里发呆
其实那是一段已废弃的铁轨
穿过一片高大的杨树林
消逝在尽头
没有呼啸声擦着树叶驶过

倒是经常会看到
拍摄婚纱照的新娘
来这里取景
站在黄昏的铁轨上
像踏上一段未知的旅程
那么多年过去了
洁白的婚纱至今还在眼前飘动

* 八福洞，韩国全州市的一个小镇。

An Unknown Journey

With 20 years gone
I still miss the rails
in my dream
in the outskirts of Eight Happy Caves*

I remember that on the summer evenings
I'd often sit there, dazed
in fact it was a section of rails in disuse
that went through a wood of tall poplar trees
and disappeared at the end
with no sound of roaring went scraping past the leaves

I'd often see
brides in wedding dresses
photographed here
they stood on the rails in the evenings
as if on an unknown journey
even though so many years have gone
the white wedding dresses seem still floating in my eyes

* Eight Happy Caves (Ba Fu Dong) or Palbok-dong, a small town in
  Jeonju-si, in Korea.

他一定后悔自己已经自杀了

晚饭后
给女儿读诗：

"十平米左右的空间
局促，潮湿，终年不见天日
我在这里吃饭，睡觉，拉屎，思考
咳嗽，偏头痛，生老，病不死
昏黄的灯光下我一再发呆，傻笑
来回踱步，低声唱歌，阅读，写诗
每当我打开窗户或者柴门
我都像一位死者
把棺材盖，缓缓推开"

"好了，你觉得如何？"
我问

"很棒，是我喜欢的菜"
她一脸惊喜，又遇到一场语言的风暴

"可惜他前几年已从富士康的楼顶跳下去了
如果还活着
他会是一个非常优秀的诗人"
我若有所失

他一定后悔自己已经自杀了
她惊讶的眼里闪过这句诗

He Must Have Wished That He Should Not Have Committed the Suicide

After dinner
I read a poem to my daughter:

'In a space of 10 square metres
narrow, damp, no light seen all the year round
here, I eat, sleep, shit, think
I cough, have migraines, I grow old but do not die of illnesses
I keep feeling dazed under the dim lights, I smile stupidly
I pace up and down, I sing in a low voice, I read, I write poetry
each time I open the window or my wooden door
I look like a dead person
gently opening the lid of a coffin'

'Okay then, what do you think?'
I said

'Wonderful, just the kind I like'
her face covered with delight, having encountered another language
storm

'But he jumped off the top of a Foxconn building a few years ago
if he were still alive
he would have become a very good poet'
I felt at a loss

'He must have wished he should never have committed the suicide'
this line flashed across her astonished eyes

人类的孩子

那天
欧阳喝得差不多了
在马路边等出租车时
他坐在马路牙子上
有些欢乐过后的
萧条
和孤寂
像一个让世界来认领的
孩子
很多时候
诗人愤怒后
脆弱的情绪，和这个世界
以及与人类微妙的关系
都表现在那种叛逆和皈依的
悖谬处境之中
越是伟大的诗人
与世界及人类的关系
越充满敌意
但他
最终还是
这个世界与人类的孩子

*此首为拾得诗，拾得自 2017 年 4 月 10 日诗人漫尘在 "求证不
  知道口炮协会" 群内对其作品《认领》的自评。

A Kid of Mankind

The other day
after he drank a bit too much
Ouyang was sitting on the edge of the road, waiting for a taxi
he was sitting there
feeling the desolation
and the solitude
after the pleasure
like a kid
for adoption
on many occasions
when a poet has vented his fury
his fragile feelings, and his subtle relationship
with this world and mankind
were all expressed in the absurd circumstances
of rebellion and conversion
the greater a poet is
the more enmity his relationship has with the world
and the humanity
but he
remines a kid
of this world and mankind

* This is a found poem, based on Man Chen's self-comment on his own
  poem, 'Adoption', posted for smashing on 10/4/2017 at KPQ WeChat
  group.

活着的骨头架

苏丹南部
已经被战争和饥
荒
折磨得
惨不忍
睹

国际人道救援机构
在苏丹境内
建立了
"苏丹生命线组织"
但还是
无法面对
这么庞大的饥
民群

一个虚弱得
站不起来的饥民
爬进
紧急避难所
他完全是
一副
活着的
骨
头
架

*此为拾得诗，链接如下：http://mp.weixin.qq.com/s/
OCnGhmxCl9i-9LX0_GPmtw

A Living Frame of Bones

South Sudan
was so ravaged
by war and star
vation
that it's horrible
to look at

Global Humanitarian Assistance
set up
'Operation Lifeline Sudan'
in Sudan
but found it impossible
to face
such masses of
hungry people

one of whom so weak
he couldn't maintain a standing position
and crept into
an emergency shelter
he was
a
complete
living frame
of
bones

* This is a found poem, found at this link: http://mp.weixin.qq.com/s/
OCnGhmxCl9i-9LX0_GPmtw

抓拍

刚出陆家嘴地铁站
一眼就看到耀眼的广告
仿佛它们在那儿等我
一个女的走过来
短时地
横在我和广告之间：
灰色的披风、细高细高的
高跟鞋
还是灰色的和带扣的
最惹眼的
是她的头发
上半部分
全染黄，只留一点点喜鹊
尾巴，全黑
我一边看
一边把感受写下来
快速完成一次
诗歌
抓拍

* 此首为拾得诗，拾得自 2017 年 4 月 16 日诗人欧阳昱在"求证
  不知道口炮协会"群内对其作品《黑的》的自评。

A Snapshot

As soon as I got out of the Lujiazui Subway Station
I saw the dazzling advertisement
as if it were waiting for me there
a woman came over
and, briefly
stood before the advertisement and I:
grey cloak, shoes with thin and high
heels
grey and strappy
the most eye-catching
was her hair
the upper part
dyed all yellow, except a magpie
tail, all black
as I looked at her
I wrote down my feelings
quickly completing
a poetic
snapshot

* This is a found poem, based on Ouyang Yu's self-comment on his
  poem, 'The Black One,' posted on KPQ on 16/4/2017.

蜣螂

城市也有低矮的窗口
踩着露水
我的生活从夜晚开始
夜空浩瀚，没有一座星辰
与我的孤独呼应

我是一枚卑微的蜣螂，喜欢
带光的事物，拜月亮为祖先
用它的偏振定位
在漆黑的夜里
以太空中的银河为导航

我喜欢动物的粪便，奉之为美食
喜欢把它们滚成小球
像怀抱珍珠般
在幽暗的角落里
为突如其来的幸福偷偷祈祷

The Dung Beetle

The city also has low windows
treading the dew
I begin my life at night
the sky is vast but there is not a single star
that echoes my solitude

I am an abject beetle and I like
things that carry light, worshipping the moon as my ancestor
positioning with its polarisation
and guided by the Milky Way in the space

I love animal dung and worship it as beautiful food
I like to roll it into tiny balls
holding them like pearls in my arms
preying by stealth for the sudden happiness
in a gloomy corner

笼罩

窗子镀满光晕
云朵停留在不远处的水坑里
像橘黄的灯
暮色里
天空威士忌一样笼罩着

牧羊人走近村庄
泥泞的路让他步履蹒跚
风抽打着满身泥水的绵羊
像弹着一床
破棉絮

更远处，是一些茅草屋
灰色的屋顶和秸秆堆闪现林间
羊圈门敞着
木门上透出隐约的光
提着马灯的女人关上了羊圈

Shrouding

The window in a halo
the cloud stopped in a puddle, not far away
like an orange lamp
at dusk
the sky shrouded like whiskey

the shepherd was walking towards the village
crippled by the muddy road
the wind lashed at the sheep dripping with muddy water
like fluffing a bed
of broken cotton wool

further away, there was a number of thatched huts
the grey roofs and the pile of straws flashed in the wood
the door of the sheep pen was open
its wooden door showed a faint light
the woman closed it, holding a horse lamp in hand

先锋……话题……继续

晚饭后回到海边民宿
男诗人们围着欧阳
一边喝茶
一边把话题扯到了先锋诗歌上
这时，艾米利亚从楼上下来
就在楼梯下面的一块绿毯上随意
躺了下来
两手举起手机
翻看着，完全一副旁若无诗人的样子
有男诗人忍不住把眼光
往那边瞟
关于先锋诗歌的话题仍在继续
艾米利亚仰躺在地上
继续翻看手机
越来越多的男诗人
不停地往她那边瞟
欧阳早已看出了端倪
便说，澳洲人就是喜欢这么随意
她才不在乎我们怎么看她呢
其实我早就想说
她随意躺在那里
远远比我们谈论的先锋诗
更先锋

The Avant-Garde...the Topic...Continued

After we got back to our seaside accommodation
the male poets were sitting around Ouyang
drinking
while talking about the avant-garde poetry
when Amelia came downstairs
and lay down on a green carpet under the stairs
just like that
mobile phone held up in her hands
swiping the screen, paying no attention to the other poets
a male poet couldn't help glancing
her way
but the topic of avant-garde poetry was continuing
and Amelia, lying faceup on the floor
went on swiping
till more and more male poets
kept glancing her way
Ouyang, having spotted it
said: Australians are like that
and she doesn't really care how we look at her
and what I had long wanted to say was that
the way she casually lay there
was far more avant-garde
than our avant-garde lip service

蹲

"你好，打扰你一分钟时间。"
他边说边在她面前
蹲下来
"放心，我不是坏人。
这是一款新型除污产品，
我给你演示一下。"
他在自己的帆布手提袋上
涂了几笔
随后用他力荐的产品
喷了几下
用抹布一擦
果然去污如新
期间，他不停地介绍着
产品的超级性能
始终保持着
蹲
的姿势
而坐在凳子上的她
从头到
尾
都没看他
一眼

Squatting

'Hi, can I have one minute from you please?'
He said as he squatted
in front of her
'Rest assured as I am not a bad person
and this is a new decontamination product
let me demonstrate how to use it'
He put a few brushes
to his own canvas handbag
then he shot a few sprays
with his strongly recommended product
when he mopped it with his rags
everything looked as new
in the meantime, he kept talking
about the superior performance of the product
consistently maintaining his
squatting
position
while she, sitting on the stool
never even looked
at him
from beginning
to the end

死亡的气息穿窗而来

此时的病房异常安静
十三楼的风拨动了一下窗帘缝
我感到某个地方也被
掀动了一下

9床的小伙子气色依旧灰暗
掉完头发的脑袋
耷拉在床头一角
10床的老余病情日渐加重
脸色酱黑。每次目光飘过他
那眼里绝望的光
令人心颤

11床又严严实实地拉上了床帘
每天这个时候
妻子和护工都会帮他擦一次身体
我曾不小心从缝隙里
看见他因长久瘫痪而长出的褥疮

她们仔细擦拭他
裸露的下半身
像一场送往天堂的仪式
我闻到病菌疯狂繁殖的味道
死亡的气息正穿窗而过来

Breaths of Death Were Coming through the Windows

Right now, the ward was eerily quiet
the wind, on the thirteenth floor, caused the seam of the window-
                                                  curtain to move
I got the feeling that somewhere else
something was also lifted

the guy in Bed 9 looked still grey
his head, all its hair shed
dropping by the side of the bed
Old Yu, in Bed 10, had a worsening condition
his face soy-sauce dark. Every time my glance drifted across him
the light of despair in his eye
made my heart shiver

Bed 11, once again, had pulled the bedcurtain tightly
at this time every day
his wife and the carer would clean his body
on one occasion, I, by accident, saw through the crack
the bedsore grown out of his long paralysis

carefully, they were wiping the lower
part of his naked body
like in a ritual of seeing him off to paradise
when I smelled the smell of the bacteria multiplying in madness
and the breaths of death were coming through the windows

回声

制造寂静的人
嗓子里埋着巨雷

把自己扩散开去
无数个我从四面回应

山坳是一只清脆的喇叭口
布满了翠绿色血管

Reverberations

The maker of quietude
has thunder buried inside his throat

when he disperses himself
countless 'I's echo from all sides

the col is a crisp bell mouth
crisscross with green blood vessels

野茱萸

顺着秋阳往山路深处走
诗人说要去看看
山里人的墓地
他说这种原始的土葬多好啊
人躺在里面，又像回到自然一样
亲切，三十年后
他也要埋到这里，与青山为伍
听流水做伴

阳光冰凉在岩石里，沿途
满是野茱萸摇晃在风里
枝头缀满珊瑚红小果子
摘下几颗，嚼一下
满嘴涩味。走在下山路上
看着他的背影
就像一棵被秋风忘却的
野茱萸

The Wild Evodia

Walking towards the depths of the mountain road along the autumnal

sun

the poet said that he was going to see
the cemetery of the mountain people
he said that the primitive earth burial was so good
as when you lie in it you will return to nature
so intimate, and, in thirty years
he would be buried here, in company with the green mountains
and the flowing waters

the sunlight was icy-cold in the rocks and the road was lined
with the wild evodia, swaying in the wind
with fruit that was coral-red
when I picked a few and chewed them
my mouth was filled with astringency. Walking down the hill
I looked at his back
looking as if it were a wild evodia
forgotten by the autumn wind

296 号

首先，它是一个男人的
自由国度，像圈养一只鹤一般
圈养着一支毛笔
可钢，可柔，有时也与一张宣纸
互换灵魂
清晨，蘸几滴鸟鸣写下
梦里酝酿好的绝句
松月明照的夜晚，蘸着
月光，写下一个中年男人
独处的旷达。当然，也有偶尔小醉
一管狼毫倾
吐不羁的狂草，隐约有狼嚎
在笔尖低啸
那是一个男人
独到深处时的狂舞
有时，那里还是一群诗人
雅聚砸诗的地方
女诗人踊跃当主厨的最佳帮手
还真有点
诗袖添香的感觉
要是来得早了
可以看到诗人漫尘和欧阳昱
站在门口抽烟论诗
一身短打的基本是欧阳
而镜片在烟雾后闪烁的
则是漫尘无疑

No. 296

First of all, it's a man's
kingdom of freedom, raising a brush
like raising a crane
hard and soft at the same time, capable, sometimes, of exchanging souls
with a piece of rice paper
in the morning, it dips in the drops of birds' calling and writes down
poetry brewed in a dream
and, on a night of pines and a bright moon, it dips
into the moonlight and writes down a middle-aged man's
broad-minded solitude. And, of course, there is occasional drunkenness
when the brush of weasel hair
spits out the wild grass, with faint howling of a wolf
at the tip of the brush
the feral dancing of a man
lonely to his depths
occasionally, it is also a place
for a group of poets to gather and smash poetry
and for the women poets to help out in the kitchen
all in good poetic company
if you come early
you'll see Manchen and Ouyang
talking, and smoking, about poetry, standing outside the door
the latter in shorts
and the one whose glasses were flickering behind the fog of smoke
must be the former, without a doubt

黑枝条

没有火光的夜晚
雨下得有些悄然、神秘

在一小块路灯里
我细数它们的声音
雨滴运动的曲线
多么迷人
像无法解开的方程

它们最终将消失在哪里？
不是这个夜晚要关心的事情

教堂离这里有点远
细雨中，我突然想做一次祷告
十二月的树赤裸着
在一根黑枝条上
我读懂了树的眼睛

Black Bough

on a night of no fire
the rain came that was quiet, mysterious

in a little spot of lamplight
I counted their sound
the curve the raindrops formed
was so captivating
like an unresolvable equation

where would they disappear in the end?
that was not the question for tonight

the church was a little far from here
in the drizzle, I had a sudden thought for prayer
the tree was naked in December
and on a black bough
I read, and understood, the tree's eyes

散漫

车子沿山路一直往上爬
突然，就到了路尽头
一片芦花
开得很漂亮
草木在阳光里有了阴影
顺着山下望去
就是海
云覆盖着蓝色海面
像一块块阴
沉的疤
渔村散落在小岛上
散漫的心
学会了抵抗风暴的力量
找一块石头坐下
看看四周
发现这里真是一个安静的角落
世界走远
我独自吹着风

Discursive

the car went up all the way, along the mountain road
till, all of a sudden, it reached the end of the road
a spread of reed catkins
was so pretty
the woods had shadows in the sun
if you looked down the mountain
there was the sea
the clouds covering the blue surface
like d
ark scars
fishing villages scattered on the little island
their discursive hearts
having learnt to resist the power of storms
I found a stone and sat down
and, looking around me
found that this was such a quiet corner
where the world had gone far
and I, alone, was blown by the wind

秀水弄 1 号

记得二十多年前
我的一个朋友
为了梦想
曾租住在这里
严格来说，那是房东
靠着自己房子的墙壁
临时搭的一个小棚子
除了放一张小床铺
基本就没有其它
空隙了。低矮、幽暗、潮湿
墙角有时还会长出
新鲜的蘑菇
他蜗居在里面
隔着 A3 纸大小的窗
打量着这座灰色小城
偶尔还写一些小诗
记得一个雨天
我敲开他的门
刚从午睡中
醒来的他
拉开门，探出他的
蜗牛脸

No. 1, Xiushui Lane

Twenty years ago, as far as I remember
a friend of mine
rented a place here
for the sake of his dream
strictly speaking, it was a small shed
that the landlord had temporarily put up
against the wall of his own property
there was no more space
except for a little
bed. Low, dark and damp
and, occasionally, fresh mushrooms
would grow out of a corner
he lived there, like in a snail
sizing up the grey town
through the A3-sized window
he would, from time to time, write small poems
I recall that on a rainy day
when I went over and knocked on his door
he, having just woken up
from his noon nap
pulled his door open, popping out his
snail face

醒来

没有安静的一刻。在急诊室
凌晨三点的走廊里
我醒来
写下两首短诗
两侧病床一溜排开
走廊被挤成一个梦，狭长、逼仄

走廊另一端
一张半醒的脸
从日光灯里
抬起来
或许那一刻，他读到了
我脸上残留的诗痕

而我关心手中的钥匙
有没有把死亡
锁在门外。我从躺椅上
撑起身，病床上
父亲还在喘
越来越接近一只衰败的
老风箱

Waking Up

Not a single moment of peace. In the emergency room
and in the 3 a.m. corridor
I woke up
and wrote two short poems
two rows of sickbeds
squeezed the corridor into a dream, narrow and long

at the other end of the corridor
a half-asleep face
raised itself
in the florescent light
perhaps, in that moment, he had read
the remaining traces of poetry, on my face

but what I was concerned with was whether the key in my hand
had not shut me
outside death. I raised myself
from the reclining chair as Father was still panting
in his sickbed
more and more approaching an old
declining bellows

漫长的午后

一条河
平静得抹去了所有脾气
那些激动的涟漪、红着脸的心跳
暗涌的激流
……
都在自省中不断磨平
收敛，彻底学会了安静

它不知道
当我站在面前时
终于找到了
模糊、晃动的
秋天的脸
就像在一面破碎的镜子里
找到了时光的碎银

杉树陪我站着
不说话
任风哗哗地吹着
一只冬瓜，顺着矮墙
爬上了树枝
它孤单地吊在那里
仿佛秋天即将敲响的丧钟……

A Long Afternoon

A river
so peaceful all its tempers were erased
with all its turbulent ripples, heart-leaps of flushed faces
hidden surging currents
...
continuously worn down in introspection
restrained and learning to be totally quiet

it didn't know, though
when I stood in front of it
I ended up finding
the blurry and swaying
face of the autumn
as if I had found the broken silver
in a broken mirror

the cedar tree stood, to keep me company
speaking no words
letting the wind blow, noisily
a winter melon climbed onto a branch
along the short wall
hanging there, singly
like a death knell, about to toll, for the autumn...

消失

也许，隐匿
是另一种

隔阂。我想做一只
晨鸟，隐于

繁枝。叫声渗进雨滴
内部。一扇等待

的窗，擦拭着黎明的铰链
我隐于枝叶，林子脆如瓷器

消失。成为瓷沿上
一滴清露

Disappearance

Possibly, hiding
is another

separation. I'd love to become a
morning bird, hiding

in the density of branches. Chirpings seeping into the insides
of the raindrops. A waiting

window, wiping the hinges of a dawn
I hide myself in the branches and leaves, the woods as crisp as porcelain

disappearing. To become a clean dew
on the edge of the porcelain

跳闸

麻将打得正酣
突然停电了
里面乱作一团
都说搞不懂
最近几天晚上
怎么老是突然停电
正好老艾要去解手
出门后
他看到老式楼道的
尽头
孤寡的老毕
正站在凳子上
哆嗦地举着
刚拔下的
保险丝

A Blown Fuse

In the middle of a mahjong game
the lights went off
everything turned upside down
and everyone complaining
wondering why there had been sudden power cuts
over the last few nights
it so happened that Old Ai was going to the loo
when he went out
he saw that at the end of the old-style
corridor
Old Bi, the widower
was standing on a stool
gingerly holding
a fuse
just removed

拎

下班路上
经过一段乡间路
一条小狗
躺在路中间
歪着头
一动不动
嘴边一团血，红得刺眼
我停车，下来
拎起它
轻放到路边樟树下
黑色身体已软成了一团
眼睛还未闭上
看它的样子
来到这个世界上
可能还不到两个月
睡觉前
我把手洗了又洗
总觉得
还拎着一个
魂

Picking Up

On my way home after work
Along a country road
A small dog
Was lying in the middle of the road
Its head turned to one side
Not moving
Its mouth in a pool of blood, so glaringly red
I pulled up my car and got out of it
Picking it up
And putting it, gently, under a roadside camphor tree
Its black body softened in a heap
Eyes not yet closed
It looked as if
It hadn't been born
For more than two months
Before I went to bed
I washed my hands again and again
Feeling as if
They were still carrying a
Soul

阻力

洗完澡后
女儿总是喜欢
照一下镜子

抬头照一下
挺胸照一下
偻背照一下
侧身照一下

"今天上体育课的时候
同学们说
胸大的
跑步时会有阻力的"

她突然甩出这么一句

Resistance

After a shower
My daughter likes
To look at herself in the mirror

She raises her head
She puffs out her chest
She bends her back
She turns around

'When I had PE classes today
my classmates said that
those with big breasts
would meet with resistance when running'

All of a sudden, she blurted out these words

掏

隔壁床老李的女儿终于来了
四十岁左右的模样
脸庞依旧精致
之前他一直说起女儿在美国
从他的言语里
我一次又一次地感受到
一个老男人的孤独
病房里静悄悄的
难得的好阳光
从窗缝里漏进来
我瞟了一眼隔壁床
只见她
正准备帮他接尿
她轻轻塞进尿壶
褪去裤头
轻轻掏出老李黑色
而软绵的根
又轻轻地
塞进了尿壶

Grabbing

Next bed, Old Li's daughter finally arrived
She looked 40-something
Her face still delicate
He had been talking about his daughter in America
From what he had said
I could, again and again, feel
An old man's loneliness
The ward remained quiet
A rare ray of good sunshine
Seeped into the seams of the window
I glanced at my next bed
And could see her
Getting ready to take his piss
Gently, she put in the bedpan
Took down his pants
And grabbed hold of Old Li's black
And soft root
Before putting it, gently
Into the pan

吃诗

酒过四巡
按惯例
原创诗歌朗诵轮番轰
炸了一圈
大家诗犹未尽
此时，安迪提议
每人限两分钟
即兴创作一首
并当场表演
最绝的是艾米利亚
她拿起诗人们事先签好
名字和日期的便条
一口咬了上去
咀嚼，咀嚼，咀嚼，咀嚼，咀嚼
一张接着
一张，一张接着一张地
吃
嚼烂的纸条
随着滚动的喉结
咽了下去
她一张接着
一张，一张接着
一张地往嘴里
塞
咀嚼，咀嚼，咀嚼，咀嚼，咀嚼
众诗人见状，惊讶着喊停
时间到
她吐出嚼烂的部分
笑着说
这不算什么

Eating Poetry

After the fourth round of liquor-drinking
And according to the customs
Reading of original poetry went off blasting
For one round
But everyone remained in high spirits
So high that Andy proposed
That each and every one of us create a poem in-situ
Within two minutes
And perform it
Amelia did a stunt
When she picked up slips of paper
With names and dates signed by the poets
Took a bite
Chewing, chewing, chewing, chewing, and chewing
One after
Another, and another
Eating
The chewed slips
Swallowing them up
As her Adam's apple rolled
She stuffed the slip
One after another
And still another
Into her mouth
Chewing, chewing, chewing, chewing, and chewing
The poets saw this, and, astonished, asked her to stop
When time was up
And she spat out the chewed parts
Saying, with a smile:
This is nothing

在澳洲时，我曾将
一小块澳小利亚的国旗
吃了下去

In Australia, I
Ate up
A small part of the National Flag of
Australia

蚊子

已是冬天
在卫生间角落里
发现一只蚊子
或许是飞累了
在这里稍作停歇
或许已经饿了几天
没力气再飞了
或许就打算在这里冬眠了
我一掌
下去
它干瘪的肚子里
没有一滴血
这突然让我想起前几天
蹲在菜场门口外
卖菜的那个老头
一块从高处砸下来
广告牌
盖住了他

The Mosquito

Winter now
In a corner of the toilet
I found a mosquito
Perhaps it was resting up
After a tiring flight
Or perhaps it had gone starving for a few days already
Unable to fly further
Or perhaps it was meaning to hibernate here now
With one slap
At it
I squashed its belly flat
But there was not a single blood
When I suddenly recalled that a few days ago
An old man selling the vegetables
Squatting outside the entrance to the vegetable market
Was covered by a
Billboard
That had come down from on high, smashing him flat

www.ingramcontent.com/pod-product-compliance
Lightning Source LLC
Chambersburg PA
CBHW020906100426

42737CB00044B/497